A Lifetime of Memories

David Hough & Keep Track Books

Dear _____

_____

_____

_____

_____

Best wishes,

_____

INTRODUCTION

This book is for you.

It's a book of questions and prompts that will help you look back and reflect on your life and all the experiences you've had. Undoubtedly, these deserve to be remembered and passed on to the next generations (if that's what you'd like to do).

Your early life was very different to present-day life and your life experiences are unique. Now is the time to write them down so that they won't get forgotten.

This book will help you tell the authentic story of your life. Here's how to use it:

- There is no deadline so write your memories at your own pace and whenever it suits you.
- Use your own words. This isn't meant to be an official autobiography, but a valuable heirloom.
- You don't have to answer the questions in any specific order.
- You don't have to answer every question or write about every topic. If there's a question that doesn't fit your life, feel free to change it to something that suits you better.
- If there's not enough space to write about something, feel free to add extra sheets as and when you need them.

In short: there are no rules. This is your book. Write about your life as you see fit.

Most importantly, enjoy the experience of looking back over your life. You will almost certainly find yourself remembering events, people and places you thought you had forgotten. Take pleasure in recalling those memories.

When you're ready, consider giving this book to your children, grandchildren or other relatives. They will cherish finding out more about you and your life. This book will be a priceless gift for them.

Enjoy the process of looking back and cherishing your life experiences!

CONTENTS

PART ONE
You and your relatives, pp. 7 – 32

Your birth ⋯ Your earliest memories ⋯ Your parents and grandparents ⋯ Your father's father ⋯ Your father's mother ⋯ More about your father's parents ⋯ Your mother's father ⋯ Your mother's mother ⋯ More about your mother's parents ⋯ More about your grandparents ⋯ Your father's siblings and their families ⋯ Your mother's siblings and their families ⋯ Your father ⋯ Your mother ⋯ Your brothers and sisters ⋯ Your relationship with the family ⋯ More memories about your relatives

PART TWO
Your childhood, pp. 33 – 46

Your first childhood home ⋯ Your other childhood homes ⋯ Everyday life in your early childhood ⋯ Childhood friends ⋯ Celebrations ⋯ Shopping ⋯ Your early schooldays ⋯ Your early school friends ⋯ Travel ⋯ More about your early childhood ⋯ Your fondest early childhood memories ⋯ More memories about your early childhood

PART THREE
Your teenage years and student life, pp. 47 – 66

Life at home ⋯ School experiences in your teenage years ⋯ Your typical school day ⋯ Memorable incidents at schools ⋯ Your friends in your teenage years ⋯ Teenage love ⋯ Your hobbies and interests ⋯ Travel ⋯ Entertainment ⋯ Part-time jobs and voluntary work ⋯ More memories about your teenage years ⋯ Leaving school ⋯ Plans for your life after school ⋯ Higher/further education ⋯ More memories about your student life

PART FOUR
Adulthood and working life, pp. 67 – 90

Your first job ⋯ Your other jobs ⋯ About your jobs ⋯ Military service ⋯ Your spouse/partner ⋯ Your engagement ⋯ Your wedding ⋯ Your honeymoon ⋯ Later marriges/partnerships ⋯ Your first home after marriage ⋯ Your later homes ⋯ Your children ⋯ Family life ⋯ Travel ⋯ Hobbies and interests ⋯ More memories about your adult life

PART FIVE
Your life today, pp. 91 – 106

Your life today ⋯ Your grandchildren ⋯ Your happiest family memories ⋯ Your happiest memories ⋯ Reflections on your life ⋯ What have you learned from your life? ⋯ More memories about your life

PART ONE

You and your relatives

When and where were you born?

Arlington, Virginia
Sept. 17, 1950

Were you born at home, in a nursing home, in a hospital or somewhere else?

Arlington Hospital

Do you know what time of day or night you came into the world?

I believe 9pm ish its on my birth certificate

What full name(s) were you given?

Nancy Lynn Howell

What reason did your parents have for the name(s) they chose for you? Was it a traditional name in your family? Or did your parents simply like it?

They just liked it Nancy was a popular name then

Can you recall any family stories relating to the time or place of your birth?

YOUR BIRTH

Was the city/town/village where you were born historically significant? For example, was it a place where something momentous happened? Did someone famous once live there?

....
....
....
....
....
....
....

How long had your parents lived there before you were born?

....
....

What was the historical time period like when you were born? Was it wartime or peacetime? Was it an age of plenty or an age of scarcity? How did world events affect your family?

....
....
....
....
....
....
....
....
....
....

YOUR EARLIEST MEMORIES

What is your earliest memory?

What images do your have of your immediate family or relatives? Does any single relative stand out? Who was it and why do you especially recall that particular person?

YOUR EARLIEST MEMORIES

Do you have any early memories of family occasions? Can you recall any weddings, anniversaries or birthday parties when your relatives came together to celebrate?

....
....
....
....
....
....
....
....
....
....

When you reflect back on your early years, what special feelings come to mind?
Was it a generally happy time for you?

....
....
....
....
....
....
....
....
....
....

YOUR PARENTS AND GRANDPARENTS

This is where you can write down the names of your parents and grandparents.
You can also add their dates of birth (and, if applicable, the dates of death).

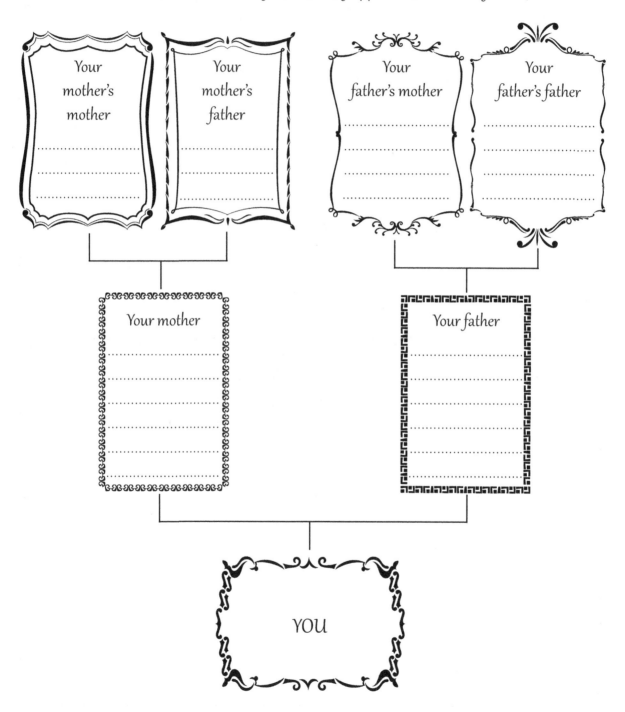

Your
mother's
mother

Your
mother's
father

Your
father's mother

Your
father's father

Your mother

Your father

YOU

YOUR FATHER'S FATHER

What did you call your father's father?

....

....

Where was he born?

....

....

....

Where did he grow up?

....

....

....

....

What was his occupation or profession?

....

....

....

What did he look like? How did he dress?

....

....

....

....

....

How did he speak? Did he have a strong accent?

....

....

....

Did he have any special mannerisms or sayings?

....

....

....

....

....

YOUR FATHER'S MOTHER

What did you call your
father's mother?

....

Where was she born?

....

....

Where did she grow up?

....

....

Did she have a job or did she look after
the home full-time?

....

....

....

What did she look like?
How did she dress?

....

....

....

....

How did she speak? Did she have a strong accent?

....

....

....

Did she have any special mannerisms or sayings?

....

....

....

....

MORE ABOUT YOUR FATHER'S PARENTS

When and where did your father's father and mother meet for the first time?

....
....
....
....
....

When and where were they married?

....
....
....
....
....

Where did they live when you were a child?

....
....
....

What was their home like?

....
....
....
....
....
....

How would you describe their relationship with each other and with the rest of the family?

....
....
....
....
....
....
....
....
....
....

YOUR MOTHER'S FATHER

What did you call your
mother's father?

Where was he born?

Where did he grow up?

What was his occupation or profession?

What did he look like? How did he dress?

How did he speak? Did he have a strong accent?

Did he have any special mannerisms or sayings?

YOUR MOTHER'S MOTHER

What did you call your
mother's mother?

....

Where was she born?

....
....
....

Where did she grow up?

....
....
....

Did she have a job or did she look after
the home full-time?

....
....
....

What did she look like?
How did she dress?

....
....
....
....

How did she speak? Did she have a strong accent?

....
....
....
....

Did she have any special mannerisms or sayings?

....
....
....
....
....

MORE ABOUT YOUR MOTHER'S PARENTS

When and where did your mother's father
and mother meet for the first time?

....
....
....
....

When and where were they married?

....
....
....
....
....

Where did they live
when you were a child?

....
....
....

What was their home like?

....
....
....
....
....
....

How would you describe their relationship with each other and with the rest of the family?

....
....
....
....
....
....
....
....
....
....
....

MORE ABOUT YOUR GRANDPARENTS

What was the historical time period like when your grandparents were young?
What was their life like then? How did their lives differ from yours?

YOUR FATHER'S SIBLINGS AND THEIR FAMILIES

Your uncles and aunts (father's side)	Their spouses/ partners	Their children (your cousins)

YOUR MOTHER'S SIBLINGS AND THEIR FAMILIES

Your uncles and aunts (mother's side)	Their spouses/ partners	Their children (your cousins)

YOUR FATHER

What do/did you call your father?

....

Where was he born?

....

Where did he grow up?

....
....
....

If your father is no longer alive, when and where did he die? Where is his grave?

....
....

What did he look like? How did he dress?

....
....
....
....

How did he speak? Did he have a strong accent?

....
....
....

Did he have any special mannerisms or sayings?

....
....
....

YOUR FATHER

What was his occupation or profession?

....

What do you know about his working life? Did he enjoy work?

....
....
....
....
....

What were his hobbies and interests? Did he do any voluntary work?

....
....
....
....
....
....
....
....
....
....

Did any wars directly affect your father? If so, in what way? How did wartime experiences affect his later life?

....
....
....
....
....
....
....
....
....

Who were your father's best friends?
What did they do when
they got together?

....
....
....
....
....
....
....
....
....
....
....
....

Was your father a healthy man?
Did he have any serious illnesses?

....
....
....
....
....
....
....
....
....
....
....
....

What is the funniest story you can recall about your father?

....
....
....
....
....
....
....
....
....

YOUR FATHER

Use this space to write about any interesting details or anecdotes about your father.
This could be something amusing or something serious that affected the rest of the family.

YOUR MOTHER

What do/did you call your mother?

....

Where was she born?

....

Where did she grow up?

....
....
....

If your mother is no longer alive, when and where did she die? Where is her grave?

....
....

What did she look like? How did she dress?

....
....
....
....

How did she speak? Did she have a strong accent?

....
....
....
....

Did she have any special mannerisms or sayings?

....
....
....
....

YOUR MOTHER

Did she have a job outside of home?

....

....

What do you know about her
working life? Did she enjoy work?

....

....

....

....

....

....

What were her hobbies and
interests? Did she do any voluntary work?

....

....

....

....

....

....

....

....

....

....

....

Did any wars directly affect your mother? If so, in what way?
How did wartime experiences affect her later life?

....

....

....

....

....

....

....

....

....

....

YOUR MOTHER

Who were your mother's best friends?
What did they do when they
got together?

....
....
....
....
....
....
....
....
....
....
....

Was your mother a healthy woman?
Did she have any serious illnesses?

....
....
....
....
....
....
....
....
....
....
....
....
....

What is the funniest story you can recall about your mother?

....
....
....
....
....
....
....
....
....
....

YOUR MOTHER

Use this space to write about any interesting details or anecdotes about your mother. This could be something amusing or something serious that affected the rest of the family.

....
....
....
....
....
....
....
....
....
....
....
....
....
....
....
....
....
....
....
....
....
....
....
....
....
....

YOUR BROTHERS AND SISTERS

The name of your brother or sister	Date of birth	Spouse/partner	Their children (your nephews and nieces)

YOUR RELATIONSHIP WITH THE FAMILY

What is your fondest memory
involving your brothers and/or sisters?

....
....
....
....
....
....
....
....
....
....
....

What is your fondest memory
about your grandparents?

....
....
....
....
....
....
....
....
....
....
....

Did you ever stay at any of your uncles or
aunts' homes? What was it like?

....
....
....
....
....
....
....
....
....
....
....
....

Which of your cousins did you feel
closest to? What memories of your time
together remain special to you?

....
....
....
....
....
....
....
....
....
....
....

MORE MEMORIES ABOUT YOUR RELATIVES

Use this space to write about any other interesting details or anecdotes about your relatives that you haven't written about yet.

PART TWO

You childhood

YOUR FIRST CHILDHOOD HOME

Where was your first childhood home?

....
....
....
....

What was it like?

....
....
....
....
....
....
....
....

What was the area like where your home was located?

....
....
....
....
....
....
....
....
....
....
....
....

Do you have any special memories of that time and/or place?

....
....
....
....
....
....
....
....
....
....

YOUR OTHER CHILDHOOD HOMES

Address of your childhood home	When did you live there?	Any special memories?

EVERYDAY LIFE IN YOUR EARLY CHILDHOOD

Before you started school, who looked after you?
Did you stay at home or did you go to a nursery or somewhere else?

....
....
....
....
....
....
....
....

What kind of food was eaten
in your childhood home?

....
....
....

What food did you enjoy most?

....
....

What food did you like least?

....
....
....

What clothes do you recall
wearing?

....
....
....

Which clothes did you like most?

....
....

Were there any clothes you hated wearing?

....
....
....

CHILDHOOD FRIENDS

What do you remember about your friends who lived nearby?
What were their names? What did they look like?

....

....

....

....

....

....

....

....

....

....

Which childhood activities did you most enjoy? What games did you and your friends play?

....

....

....

....

....

....

....

....

....

....

....

CELEBRATIONS

Tell about the earliest birthday celebration you can recall.

....
....
....
....
....
....

What presents were you given?

....
....
....
....
....

Tell about the earliest Christmas (or other religious celebration) you can recall.

....
....
....
....
....

What presents did you receive?

....
....
....
....

SHOPPING

When and where did you go shopping with your parents?

....

....

....

What sort of things did your parents buy there?

....

....

....

Which shops or stores did you most enjoy visiting?

....

....

....

Did you get to choose anything in those shops? If so, what?

....

....

....

If you were given money, what did you buy with it?

....

....

....

How much did those items cost?

....

....

....

YOUR EARLY SCHOOLDAYS

What was the name of
your first school? Where was it?

....
....
....

What did the building look like?

....
....
....

How did you travel to school? Was it
by bus, car, bicycle or did you walk?
Who went with you?

....
....

What do you remember about
the meals at school?

....
....
....
....
....
....
....
....
....
....
....
....

Which teacher(s) remain most strongly in your mind?
What were they called and what did they teach?

....
....
....

Why do you remember those teachers? What was it about them that made them memorable?

....
....
....

YOUR EARLY SCHOOLDAYS

What lessons did you most enjoy?
What made them so enjoyable?

What lessons did you least like?
Why did you not enjoy them?

Which school sports did you most enjoy?

Which school sports did you least enjoy?

Did you ever get up to any mischief in your early schooldays? Now is your chance to make a full confession!

YOUR EARLY SCHOOL FRIENDS

Who were your friends in your early schooldays? What were they like?

....
....
....
....
....
....
....
....
....
....

Who was your best friend?

....
....

What special memories of that person remain with you?

....
....
....
....
....
....
....
....
....

What memorable things did you and your school friends do together outside school time? For example, did you attend any clubs or summer camps together?

....
....
....
....
....
....
....
....
....
....

TRAVEL

What is your earliest memory of a trip away from home? How old were you then?

....
....

Where did you go?

....
....

Who went with you?

....
....

What did you do there?

....
....

Do you recall any other memorable trips away from home?
Where did you go and what did you do there?

....
....
....
....
....
....
....
....
....
....

MORE ABOUT YOUR EARLY CHILDHOOD

Which toys did you most enjoy playing with?

....
....
....

What games did you enjoy playing with your brothers and sisters?

....
....
....
....
....

Did you have an imaginary friend? What was his/her name?

....
....
....

What pets did you have? What were their names?

....
....
....
....

What was the naughtiest thing you ever did as a child?

....
....
....
....
....

How did your parents react if you were naughty? What did they do if you were <u>very</u> naughty?

....
....
....
....

YOUR FONDEST EARLY CHILDHOOD MEMORIES

What are the early childhood memories that bring you the greatest happiness?

MORE MEMORIES ABOUT YOUR EARLY CHILDHOOD

Use this space to write about any other interesting details or anecdotes about
your early childhood that you haven't written about yet.

PART THREE

Teenage years
and student life

LIFE AT HOME

How did you get on with your parents in your teenage years?

What kinds of activities did you do together as a family?

How did you get on with your siblings?

What chores did you do at home as a teenager?

LIFE AT HOME

What kinds of insecurities did you
have as a teenager?

Looking back at your teenage self, how
would you describe yourself?

How did you dress as a teenager?

What did you usually do at weekends?

SCHOOL EXPERIENCES IN YOUR TEENAGE YEARS

What was the name of
your school? Where was it?

....

....

....

What did the building look like?

....

....

....

How did you travel to school? Was it by
bus, car, bicycle or did you walk? Who
went with you?

....

....

....

What do you remember about
the meals at school?

....

....

....

....

....

....

....

....

....

....

....

Which teacher(s) remain most strongly in your mind?
What were they called and what did they teach?

....

....

....

Why do you remember those teachers? What was it about them
that made them memorable?

....

....

....

SCHOOL EXPERIENCES IN YOUR TEENAGE YEARS

What lessons did you most enjoy?
What made them so enjoyable?

....
....
....
....
....
....
....
....
....
....

What lessons did you least like?
Why did you not enjoy them?

....
....
....
....
....
....
....
....
....
....

Which school sports did you most enjoy?

....
....
....
....
....

Which school sports did you least enjoy?

....
....
....
....
....

Did you ever get into any trouble at
school? What did you do?

....
....
....
....
....
....
....
....
....
....

YOUR TYPICAL SCHOOL DAY

What was a typical school day like for you and your classmates? What was your schedule? How did you feel about school and what kinds of thoughts did you have?

MEMORABLE INCIDENTS AT SCHOOL

What school incident(s) do your recall in your teenage years? These
may have involved you, your friends or your teachers. What happened?

....
....
....
....
....
....
....
....
....
....
....
....
....
....
....
....
....
....
....
....
....
....
....
....

YOUR FRIENDS IN YOUR TEENAGE YEARS

Who were your friends in your
teenage years? What were they like?

....
....
....
....
....
....
....
....
....
....
....

Who was your best friend?

....
....

What special memories of that person
remain with you?

....
....
....
....
....
....
....

What memorable things did you and your friends do together?
For example, did you attend any clubs or summer camps together?

....
....
....
....
....
....
....
....
....

TEENAGE LOVE

Who was your first teenage crush? How old were you?
What was he/she like? What happened?

....
....
....
....
....
....
....
....
....
....
....

Did you have a boyfriend/girlfriend when you were a teenager? What was he/she like?
How did the relationship start? How long were you together?

....
....
....
....
....
....
....
....
....
....
....

YOUR HOBBIES AND INTERESTS

What hobbies did you have during your teenage years? Did you belong to any clubs or
organizations? Were you genuinely passionate about these hobbies or
did you take part because your parents or friends wanted you to?

....
....
....
....
....
....
....
....

What kinds of things were you interested in?

....
....
....
....
....
....

Can you recall a memorable hobby-related event or incident?
This could be something funny or something terrible. What happened?

....
....
....
....
....
....

TRAVEL

Did you make any family trips during your teenage years? Which places did you visit?

....

....

....

....

....

What did you like doing when you were away from home?

....

....

....

....

Do you recall a trip that was particularly memorable?
Where did you go? What happened?

....

....

....

....

....

....

....

....

....

....

ENTERTAINMENT

What kind of music did you listen to?

What singers or groups most appealed to you? Did you go to their concerts?

What books did you enjoy reading?

Did you read any magazines?
Which one(s) did you most enjoy?

ENTERTAINMENT

Which TV and/or radio shows did you enjoy? Why did those particular shows appeal to you?

....
....
....
....
....
....
....
....
....
....
....
....
....
....
....

What was the first movie you ever saw in the cinema?

....
....
....

How often did you go to the cinema? Which movies did you most enjoy?

....
....
....
....
....

PART-TIME JOBS AND VOLUNTARY WORK

Did you have a part-time job while you were at school?
If so, what did you do and where did you work?

How did you spend the money that you received?

Did you do any voluntary work during your teenage years?
If so, what did you do? How did it make you feel?

MORE MEMORIES ABOUT YOUR TEENAGE YEARS

Use this space to write about any other interesting details or anecdotes about
your teenage years that you haven't written about yet.

LEAVING SCHOOL

What grades did you achieve when you left school?

How did you feel on your last day?

Have you stayed in touch with the friends you had as a teenager? How often do you meet?

What is the most valuable thing you learned at school?

PLANS FOR YOUR LIFE AFTER SCHOOL

What did you want to do when you left school?

....

....

What inspired you to think about a particular career?

....

....

....

What kind of career guidance were you given and by whom?

....

....

....

What other kinds of aspirations did you have? This could be about family life
or something related to your hobbies and interests. Did they come true?

....

....

....

....

....

....

....

....

....

....

HIGHER/FURTHER EDUCATION

What higher or further education courses did you take? This could be academic, technical or work related.

At what educational institution(s) did you study?

What subjects did you study?

Did you have a part-time job while you were studying? What did you do?

HIGHER/FURTHER EDUCATION

How was student life for you?

....

....

....

....

....

....

....

....

....

....

....

....

What qualification(s) did you gain?

....

....

....

To what use did you put your qualification(s)? How did they help you in later life?

....

....

....

....

MORE MEMORIES ABOUT YOUR STUDENT LIFE

Use this space to write about any other interesting details or anecdotes about
your student life that you haven't written about yet.

PART FOUR

Adulthood
and working life

YOUR FIRST JOB

How old were you when you started work?

....

....

....

Where was your place of work?

....

....

....

....

....

What was your first proper job and
what were your tasks and responsibilites?

....

....

....

....

....

....

....

....

....

....

....

....

What was your first boss like?

....

....

....

....

How did you feel about that job?
Did you like it or hate it?

....

....

....

....

....

....

....

....

....

....

....

....

How did you get this job?

....

....

....

....

YOUR OTHER JOBS

Date	Job title	Name of company/organization
From To		
From To		
From To		
From To		
From To		
From To		
From To		
From To		
From To		
From To		
From To		
From To		
From To		
From To		

ABOUT YOUR JOBS

How did your jobs affect your home life?

Did you have any good friends at work? Do you still stay in touch with them?

Which job did you like the most? Why?

Which job did you like the least? Why?

What was your daily routine during your working life?

MILITARY SERVICE

Did you take part in military service? If so, which service
did you join: army, navy or air force?

....

....

....

When was it?

....

....

What was your rank?

....

....

Did you serve in any wars? If so,
where and for how long?

....

....

....

....

What was your role?

....

....

....

....

....

Write about your experiences
in the military.

....

....

....

....

....

....

....

....

....

....

....

....

YOUR SPOUSE/PARTNER

When did you meet your future spouse/partner? How old were you?

....
....

Where did you meet? Was it a date or did you meet at school or at work?

....
....
....
....
....
....
....

What attracted you to your future spouse/partner? What was special about him/her?

....
....
....
....
....
....
....
....
....
....
....
....

YOUR ENGAGEMENT

What do you remember about the moment you agreed to spend your lives together?

When and where did you seal this commitment to one another?

How did you feel afterwards?

....
....
....
....
....
....
....
....
....

How did you celebrate your
engagement?

....
....
....
....
....
....
....
....
....
....
....

What special memories do you have
of the time you were engaged?

....
....
....
....
....
....
....
....
....
....

YOUR WEDDING

When were you married?

....
....
....
....

Where were you married?

....
....
....
....
....
....

What did the wedding dress look like?

....
....
....
....
....
....
....
....
....
....
....
....
....

Who were the bridesmaids?

....
....
....
....
....

Who was the best man?

....
....
....

How many guests were there?
Who were they?

....
....
....
....
....
....
....
....
....
....
....
....
....

Tell about your wedding day. Can you remember any
memorable speeches or something funny that happened?

....
....
....
....
....
....
....
....
....
....
....
....
....
....
....
....
....
....
....
....
....
....
....
....

YOUR HONEYMOON

Where did you go on your honeymoon? How long did you stay there?

....

....

Was there something special about the place?

....

....

....

....

What memories or funny moments will you always remember about your honeymoon?

....

....

....

....

....

....

....

....

....

....

....

....

....

....

....

....

....

....

LATER MARRIAGES/PARTNERSHIPS

Did you have more than one spouse/partner? Use this space to write about your new
relationship(s). How did you meet? What attracted you to your new partner(s)?
Did you have a traditional wedding or some other celebration?

YOUR FIRST HOME AFTER MARRIAGE

Where was your first home
after marriage?

....
....
....

What was it like?

....
....
....
....
....
....

What was the area like where
your home was located?

....
....
....
....
....
....
....
....
....
....

What special memories do you have of living in that home?

....
....
....
....
....
....
....
....
....
....

YOUR LATER HOMES

Address	When did you live there?	Any special memories?

YOUR CHILDREN

Name of your child	Date of birth	Place of birth	What was the birth like?

YOUR CHILDREN

Name of your child	What was he/she like as a baby?	What was he/she like as a teenager?

FAMILY LIFE

What did your children call you
when they were young?

....
....
....
....
....

What do your children call you now?

....
....
....
....
....

Did your family have any pets? What
were they and when did you have them?

....
....
....
....
....
....
....
....
....
....
....
....
....

What kind of transport did you use? What cars, motorbikes or boats did you have?
What special memories do you have of those vehicles?

....
....
....
....
....
....
....
....
....
....
....
....
....

Did you stay at home any length of time to look after your children
when they were babies and/or toddlers? What were the days like?

FAMILY LIFE

What did you do when the children were at school?

What makes you proud of your children? This could be, for example, their achievements, special occasions or what they are like as people.

FAMILY LIFE

What funny stories can you tell about your children?

Which places did you visit with the whole family?

....

....

....

....

Did you ever travel with just your spouse/partner? Where did you go?

....

....

....

....

....

....

....

Do you recall a trip that was particularly memorable? Where did you go?
What happened?

....

....

....

....

....

....

....

HOBBIES AND INTERESTS

What hobbies did you have during your adult life? Were they the same hobbies
that you had as a teenager or did you discover new interests?

....
....
....
....
....
....
....
....

What activities did you most enjoy doing in your leisure time?

....
....
....
....
....
....
....

Did you have any hobbies that you shared with your whole family? If so, what were they?

....
....
....
....
....
....

HOBBIES AND INTERESTS

Did you attend any educational courses, either just for fun or to learn something that would help you in your job? What were these courses and what subjects or skills did you study?

....

....

....

....

....

....

....

....

....

Did you do any voluntary work? What was it? Who did you help and how often?

....

....

....

....

....

....

....

....

....

....

....

....

MORE MEMORIES ABOUT YOUR ADULT LIFE

Use this space to write about any other interesting details or anecdotes about your adult life that you haven't written about yet.

PART FIVE

Your life today

YOUR LIFE TODAY

Where do you live now and with whom?

....
....
....
....

How long have your lived there?

....
....

What is the area like where your home is located?

....
....
....
....
....
....
....
....

What is your home like?

....
....
....
....
....
....
....
....
....

YOUR LIFE TODAY

At what age did you retire from full-time work?

....

....

How did you feel about retiring?

....

....

....

....

....

How do you fill your days in retirement? Do you have a part-time job?
Do you volunteer? What hobbies do you have? What else do you do?

....

....

....

....

....

....

....

....

....

....

....

....

....

....

....

YOUR GRANDCHILDREN

Name of your child	Names of your children's children and their dates of birth

YOUR GRANDCHILDREN

How did you first hear about
becoming a grandparent?

....
....
....
....
....
....

How did it make you feel?

....
....
....

What does being a grandparent
mean to you?

....
....
....
....
....
....
....
....
....
....
....

Do you treat your grandchildren differently from how you treated your own children
when they were young? If so, in what way?

....
....
....
....
....
....
....
....
....

YOUR HAPPIEST FAMILY MEMORIES

Looking back on your life, what is your fondest memory relating to your spouse/partner?

What is your fondest memory relating to your children?

YOUR HAPPIEST FAMILY MEMORIES

What is your fondest memory relating to your grandchildren?

What is your fondest memory relating to a family event or trip?

YOUR HAPPIEST MEMORIES

What is your fondest memory of a personal achievement?

What are you most grateful for when you look back on your life?

REFLECTIONS ON YOUR LIFE

What do you think and feel about your life at the moment?
How is it better or worse than your working life?

....
....
....
....
....
....
....
....
....
....

What beliefs do you hold these days? Think about your religious, ideological and/or
political views. Are they the same as when you were younger or have they changed?

....
....
....
....
....
....
....
....
....
....
....
....

What do you like about the modern world?

....
....
....
....
....
....
....
....
....
....
....
....

Now be honest and tell what you really dislike about the modern world.

....
....
....
....
....
....
....
....
....
....
....
....

REFLECTIONS ON YOUR LIFE

Was there someone you were close to who had a particularly strong influence
on your life? Who was it and in what way was he/she important?

....
....
....
....

If you met that person now, what would you say to him/her?

....
....
....

Was there someone you never met who nonetheless had a strong influence
on you? Who was it and in what way was he/she important?

....
....
....
....

If you met that person now, what would you say to him/her?

....
....
....
....

REFLECTIONS ON YOUR LIFE

If you could go back in time and change something about your life, what would it be?

....
....
....
....
....
....
....
....
....
....
....

Looking back on your life, what difficulties did you overcome, and how did you do it?

....
....
....
....
....
....
....
....
....
....

REFLECTIONS ON YOUR LIFE

Where did you find comfort when you most needed it?

If you were to write your own epitaph, what would it say?

WHAT HAVE YOU LEARNED FROM YOUR LIFE?

You have a lifetime of experience behind you and you will have learned so much from it.
If someone asked you what wisdom you have gained over the years, what would you say?
Use these two pages to write down any advice that you would like to pass on.

WHAT HAVE YOU LEARNED FROM YOUR LIFE?

MORE MEMORIES ABOUT YOUR LIFE

Use this space to write about any other interesting details or anecdotes about your life that you haven't written about yet.

NOTEBOOKS AND JOURNALS

I Remember That is a guided memory journal for recording personal memories of events from 1945 to 2000. It contains questions and prompts that will take you down memory lane and help you recall experiences relating to what was happening in the world.

Both the UK and the US editions are available in either standard or large print
Find out more at **www.lusciousbooks.co.uk/i-remember-that**

Password notebooks – Are you struggling to keep track of all your passwords and user-names? Now you can keep all those important website addresses and login details in one notebook!

See all the cover options at
www.lusciousbooks.co.uk/password-notebooks

Want to keep your Christmas card addresses in one place and track to whom you've sent cards and from whom you've received them? With this handy **Christmas card address book** you can!

See all the cover options at
www.lusciousbooks.co.uk/christmas-card-address-books

Visit www.lusciousbooks.co.uk to find out more

ABOUT THE CREATORS OF THIS BOOK

David Hough

David Hough was born in Cornwall and spent forty years working as an air traffic controller before retiring early in 2003 and becoming a writer. He has written over 30 novels and now lives with his wife in Dorset, on the south coast of England.

www.TheNovelsofDavidHough.com

Books by David Hough

Non-fiction
Grandad's Quiz Book
A Route Map to Novel Writing Success

Danger in the Sky aviation thrillers
Prestwick
Heathrow
Dead Reckoning

Secret Soldiers of World War I spy thrillers
In Foreign Fields
In Line of Fire

Adventures in Cornwall series
In the Shadow of a Curse
In the Shadow of Disgrace
In the Shadow of Deception

The Family Legacy series
The Legacy of Shame
The Legacy of Secrets
The Legacy of Conflict

Keep Track Books

Keep Track Books is Luscious Books' notebook and journal series. Currently the following notebooks and journals are available:

- Password notebooks
- Christmas card address books
- Blank sheet music
- Gratitude journals
- Dream journals
- Gone but not forgotten - What to do after I'm dead
- What to do with my business after I'm dead
- Notebooks for boring meetings (these contain Sudoku puzzles to keep you amused)

Please visit **www.lusciousbooks.co.uk/ keep-track-books** to find out more.

Luscious Books

Luscious Books is an independent publishing house specialising in puzzle books, activity books, cookbooks for special diets, notebooks and journals.

Its fiction imprint, Cloudberry, publishes commercial fiction.

Explore books at:
www.lusciousbooks.co.uk
www.cloudberrybooks.co.uk